"I ASK"
A Book About Consent

Written By
Sherry Stone Yetter

#NOMEANSNO
#QUESTIONSARECOOL
#KIDSHEALTHYBOUNDARIES
#KIDSCONSENTMATTERS

"I ASK" All About Consent
published by Sunflower Books LLC
www.sunflowerbooksllc.com
ISBN: 978-1-7358619-1-3 (paperback)
First Edition, 2021
Text copyright @ Sherry Stone Yetter 2021
Illustration copyright @ Sherry Stone Yetter 2021

Written by Sherry Stone Yetter
Photos /Illustrations by Sherry Stone Yetter and Gregg Yetter
Edited/Designed by Gregg Yetter

****

This book was purposefully published during April which is also Sexual Assault Awareness and Prevention Month. A portion of the proceeds from the sale of each book will be donated to support victim advocacy, education efforts, and justice for victims.

I also want to thank everyone who has ever stood up for or advocated for a victim of child or adult sexual abuse. No one should ever know that pain. I believe that by using our collective voices, we can and will do better as a society.

****

Illustrations were created using Procreate and Canva. Canva artists include: Leremy Gan, blueringmedia, Moose, Haluk Kohserli, lineartestpilot2, Yayayoyo, Marmalade Moon, sketchify, BNPDesignStudio, puruanstock, djvstock, aidenopoly, icons8, yupiramos, putrabahagiaicons, ivandesign, NotionPic, Oneywhystudio. Thank you.

ISBN: 978-1-7358619-1-3

9 781735 861913

*****

This book is dedicated to my first grandchild Jody Lynn aka "Kiwi" and to her GreggPa. Kiwi first inspired me to write this very important story and then GreggPa is the one who said I needed to share it with you. From the mouths of babes began an incredible journey and I look forward to seeing where she inspires me to go next.

I ASK A Book About Consent is loosely based on a conversation Jody and I had about my job as a victim advocate and how I help people recover from trauma. It is my most fervent wish that she and every other child never know anything but consent and respect.

*****

Do you have a nickname?

I do, mine is Kiwi.

Kiwi,

you know,

like the green fruit

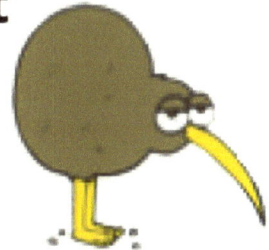

or the bird.

My grandparents gave me that nickname
when I was little. They have nicknames too.
I call them GiGi and GreggPa.

My Mom says I ask a lot of questions.

I think that is a good thing to do because my GreggPa says it will help keep me out of trouble all my life.

I don't like to get into trouble or be put into time-out, do you?

My GiGi says I ask a lot of questions too but I think some of them make her cranky.

You know, cranky, like when my baby sister Phoebe needs a nap because that is usually when GiGi says I get on her "last nerve."

GiGi says that a lot especially when we are in the car and I ask her,

"Are we there yet?
Are we there yet?
Are we there yet?"
over and over and over!

Sometimes I do that just to see what kind of face she is going to make!

It makes me giggle when she says I am *ornery* (awr-nuh-ree) like my Poppa Brandon or *incorrigible* (in-kawr-i-juh-buhl) like my Aunt Clarissa.

GiGi always says that with a smile so I think that must be a good thing.

GiGi says that asking questions is how adults and kids know...

What they can and cannot do.

My Mom says a good question to ask is...

"Can I give you a hug?"

I think this is a great question.

I like hugs and I really like it when people ask me first.

My GiGi gives the best hugs ever!
When she asks if she can give me a hug I always say "Yes." GiGi's hugs make me feel all warm inside.

One day, GreggPa got a big chalkboard out so we could write a list of questions that I should ask others.

He called it a *permission* (pur-mish-uhn) board but GiGi called it a *"let's-keep-Kiwi-safe-board."*

Together, we painted the board blue. I added lots of red, purple, blue, pink, yellow, and green polka dots until the board was covered.

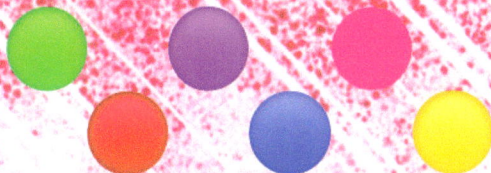

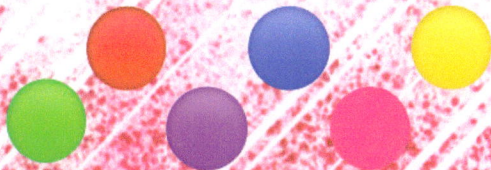

As we worked on the board, GiGi asked what questions I thought I should ask people and then what questions people should ask me?

Together we came up with a list and then she wrote them on the board.

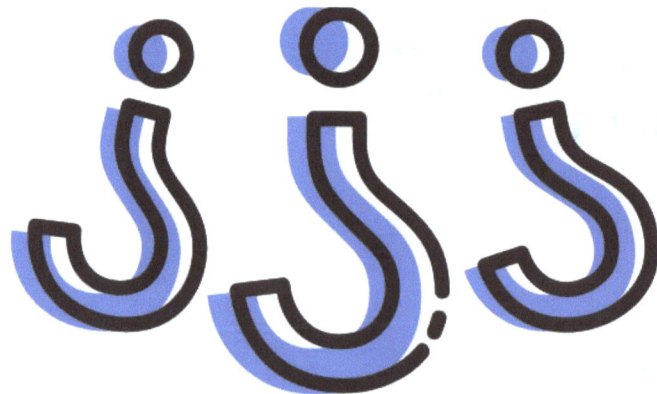

Kiwi's Respectful Questions Board

I must ask permission

To go somewhere
To give a hug
To borrow something
To touch someone else
To touch something that isn't mine
To kiss someone
To share a secret

Out of respect for others I will ask questions and hope they ask me respectful questions too.

My favorite question on the board is...
"I know I must ask *permission* to share a secret." I can keep a good secret, I promise. I really, really can.

Just ask GiGi about her birthday party last year. I knew all day long
it was a surprise and I
didn't spill the beans.

Everyone sure was surprised!

When answering a question, GiGi says it is very important for me to say,

"Yes," "No," "Yes, please" or "No, thank you."

This way the person asking the question hears your answer.

Sometimes I forget... and nod my head when answering questions, but she reminds me to also say my answer out loud.

I like it when she reminds me. It helps me learn.

As I was leaving, GreggPa asked me if I wanted a hug and I said, "No, thank you GreggPa."

GreggPa said, "Okay, I *respect* your answer."

"*Re-spect*? I said curiously, "What does that mean?"

GreggPa replied, "Well, I asked if you wanted a hug and you said 'No', so that means I will respect your answer and will not give you a hug without your *permission*. This is what we talked about. It's called respecting a person's *boundaries* (boun-duh-rees)."

"Hmm," I wondered curiously,

"But what if I want a hug tomorrow ? "

Remember,
       I said I ask a LOT of questions.

"If you do not want a hug say, 'No' or 'No, thank you' or even 'No thank you, maybe later'. This way the person knows you do not *consent* to a hug right now," said GreggPa.

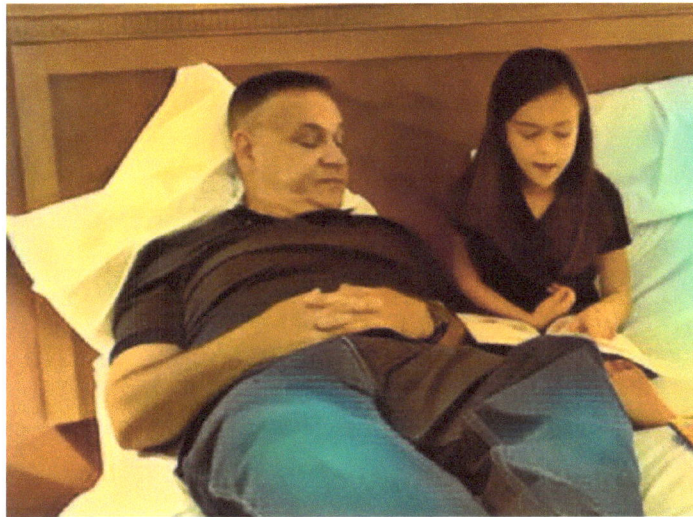

GreggPa saw the confused look on my face, and asked if I knew what *consent* meant? I shook my head no, looked at GiGi, giggled, and then I said, "No," to GreggPa out loud.

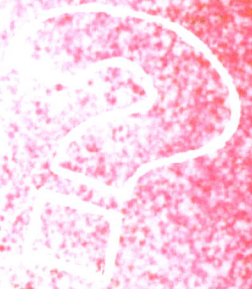

GiGi explained that *consent* is just like asking for *permission* to do or touch something. Then GreggPa told me it is super important that we never force anyone to do something they do not want to do.

"Like give them a hug or a kiss?" I said. "YESSSSSSSSSS," GiGi and GreggPa exclaimed together, "You got it!"

GreggPa said, "It's okay to say 'No' even if you said 'Yes' the day before. Sometimes we do not want to hug someone and that is okay. We should always *respect* a person's answer, no matter what."

Then, we practiced ways for me to say no.

I don't feel
like it right now.

Maybe
tomorrow?

No, thank you.
Not today.

It's OK, I
understand!

How about we
fist bump?

Ask me
again later?

Nah, I'm
good.

GiGi says we ask for *consent* all the time and may not realize that we are doing it. She also said that sometimes the answer is "Yes" and sometimes the answer is "No." GiGi said *consent* questions are like *permission* questions because we are asking to be able to do or have something.

May I have a sucker please?

Do you want to play with me?

Do you want to sit on the bus with me?

May I hold your toy?

Can we play together at recess?

Will you share your crayons with me?

May I watch videos on YouTube?

Would you like to come to my house?

May I stay up late Mom?

"Ohhhh", I said, "So, asking for *consent* to do something is like asking for... umm... what's that word ... oh yeah... *permission* (per-mish-uhn). Am I saying that word right?"

GiGi smiled, and said, "yes" while nodding her head in agreement.

"Respecting someone and their *boundaries* means that you should always ask if it is ok to touch them," GiGi said as we looked at pictures of me and GreggPa on her phone.

"So, that would mean GreggPa consented to me messing up his hair that one time?" I said as I giggled remembering the mohawk I gave him.

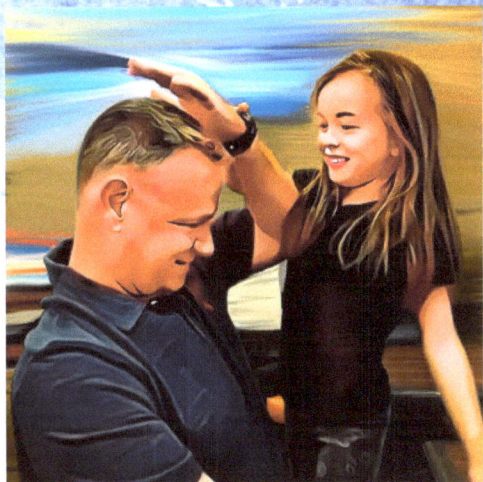

"Did you ask permission first?" GiGi said. I nodded yes, "Oh, yes, I did. You know how he is about his hair." And then we both giggled.

That is when I told GiGi about the time Uncle Alex didn't want to play hide-and-go-seek with me. I told him that was OK and went to play with Aunt Crissy instead.

GiGi smiled and said, "Yes, you respected his answer and his *boundaries*. That is exactly how you handle it. Good girl!"

Then GreggPa said, "By remembering to ask for *consent* and by learning to honor the answer we receive, we show *respect* for a person's *boundaries*."

"Aha," I thought.

I grinned as I looked at GiGi and GreggPa and asked, "Do you *consent* to stopping at the candy store on our way home?"

Guess what? They said, "Yes" and I got a gigantic pixie stick.

A Parental Guide:

Teachable Moments

TALKING POINTS
"I Ask: All About Consent"

Key Words: Respect, Consent, Boundaries, and Permission

Consent, a word that has had such an impact on adult behavior. Many of us learned about healthy personal boundaries too late and it negatively impacted our lives. What would have happened if we were taught boundaries, respect, consent, and advocacy as children? Would our lives have been different? Would our interactions with others have been different? Probably.

As parents, teachers, grandparents, and adults, it is important we model appropriate ways in asking for consent in both action and in words. This section is meant to support parents and adults as they assist a child with this type of discussion. It is intended to be a educational beginning on this difficult topic. ** Please note that while the principal character in this book is female the message in this book is applicable to all children.

Consent. Understand that teaching a child about consent is equally about them asking for consent; learning to respect another person's boundaries; that consent can change; and, further, that when we do not respect individual boundaries there are consequences to our choices.

No Pressure. No one should ever feel pressured to do something that they are uncomfortable with and that goes for kids too!

Setting Physical Boundaries. Encourage children to learn to identify body parts in age appropriate terms. Parents can begin by teaching their child about respecting physical boundaries by modeling consent and not tickling, kissing, or hugging a child when they say 'no' or 'stop'. Once that concept is mastered you can then move on to personal boundaries or more specific messages such as "no means no" or "is it ok if I…" before they touch someone.

Sharing. Be sure you to tell the child it is more than OK to share things with you or with a trusted adult such as a teacher or principal, etc. This is the child's beginning to identify the need to advocate for self and others along with the ability to identify trusted individuals. Sometimes a child may fear making an adult upset because they have been told something bad will happen if they tell anyone. Thank them for trusting you with this important information.

Supportive/Caring. Always be encouraging and supportive and let them know you are there for them no matter what has happened. It is also important to tell the child that is not at fault if someone has touched them inappropriately or if something bad has happened.

Gut Feelings. Talk to your child about "gut feelings" and explain that every-once-in-a-while we may get a weird feeling inside and that we may not be able to explain why we feel that way. All we know is that something feels "off" or uncomfortable or that something just doesn't feel quite right. Teach your child to respect those "gut feelings" when they happen, who to communicate with that they have these feelings, and how they should respond in those moments.

Build Value. Teach your child that learning to recognize a "gut feeling" is one way that our inner voice tells us to be careful or cautious or even sometimes to stop what we are doing or what we are seeing because it isn't right. Assure your child of the importance in trusting these feelings and explain that even adults trust their "gut feelings" because it helps to protect us or keep us safe.

Secrets. Be prepared to help kids tell the difference between good secrets, surprises, and bad secrets. Explain that there are good secrets we can keep like who is getting what present for Christmas or when we are invited to a surprise birthday party but that there are also secrets that are harmful and those secrets are the kind we shouldn't keep them to ourselves. Teach them that some secrets can hurt someone (be prepared to provide examples) and that they should tell you immediately.

Modeling Behaviors. Remember that our children learn by watching how we interact with other children and adults. When children see parents or adults yelling or hitting each other they will get the message that violence is how you get your way or how you should communicate.

Importance of "Yes". Teach your child how to give consent in an enthusiastic, active, visible and an undeniably "yes" way.

Importance of "No". Teach your child how NOT to give consent in a firm, visible, active, and an undeniably "no" manner.

Teachable Moments. I highly recommend using teachable moments, such as these, to introduce to and to talk about topics such as consent, respect, boundaries, and consequences with your child. Topical questions are suggested below to help get you started.

- Ask a child to identify the times they should ask for consent.
- Ask a child to identify the times that others should ask them for consent.
- Ask a child to identify trusted adults such as teachers, parents, etc.
- Ask a child to describe how their actions might make another person feel if they don't respect their answer? (For example: Giving a person a hug or a kiss after they said they didn't want one.)
- Tell the child it is OK to ask questions and remind them that asking questions is how we all learn, even adults.

About the Author

Sherry Stone Yetter is a trained and credentialed Victim Advocate and Subject Matter Expert on the topics of Sexual Assault and Sexual Harassment Victim Advocacy. She has degrees in Social Science and Education and has advanced degrees in Organizational Leadership and Servant Leadership.

Sherry is a Mom of two children and two fur babies. She is also the wife of a retired United States Marine aka "GreggPa" and is "GiGi" to three of the most amazing grandchildren in the world.

Sherry grew up in Iowa and credits her strong faith, fortitude, resilience, and ability to persevere in the face of overwhelming obstacles to her upbringing; and to those who also taught her how to love, to be kind, and the positivity of respecting others. Sherry's goals are to spend her life being a positive, helping influence for others. Oh, and to continue writing new books.

Sherry Stone Yetter's Other Books

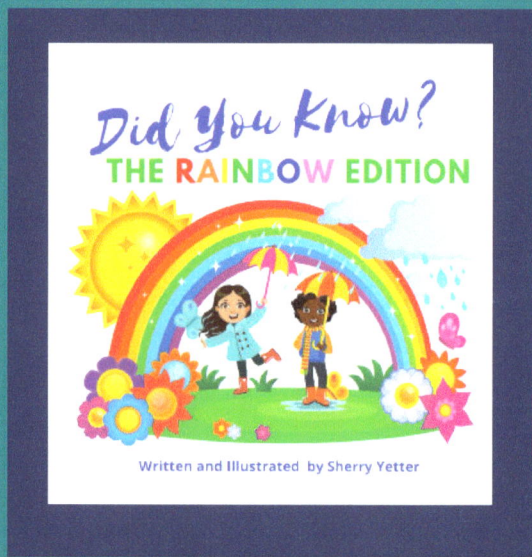

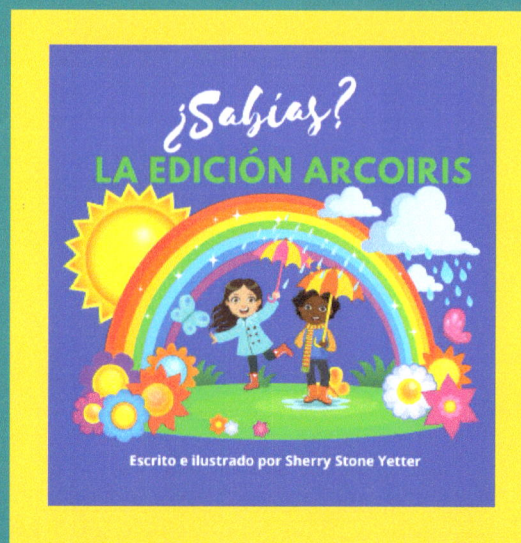

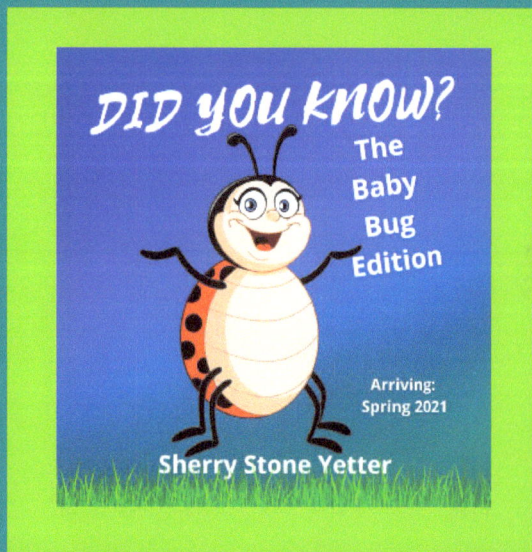

Did You Know?
THE RAINBOW EDITION

Written and Illustrated by Sherry Yetter

¿Sabías?
LA EDICIÓN ARCOIRIS

Escrito e ilustrado por Sherry Stone Yetter

DID YOU KNOW?
The Baby Bug Edition

Arriving: Spring 2021

Sherry Stone Yetter

Social Media

@mysunflowerbooks

@SunflowerBooksPublishing

@BooksSunflower

www.SunflowerBooksLLC.com

www.ingramcontent.com/pod-product-compliance
Lightning Source LLC
LaVergne TN
LVHW072108070426
835509LV00002B/67